WHERE DO OUR HEARTS GO

SREEHARI KN

To the ones who loved and left,
To the ones who stayed and held my hand,
And to those I have yet to meet on this journey of love and
longing.

Gratitude to my Marupakuthi…
And to the people who stood by me through every storm and
silence.

With love,
Sreeeeee

Contents

Contents

Contents

Preface

This book is a journey of the heart. It's about love, loss, and the quiet strength we discover in ourselves when we think we've lost everything. The words here are a reflection of the feelings I've carried with me through the hardest times moments of deep pain and moments of surprising peace. These poems and thoughts are not just mine; they belong to anyone who has ever loved, lost, or felt broken and found themselves again.

This is for anyone who has ever wondered if they could ever heal after heartbreak, or if they would ever be okay again. I've learned that healing isn't something we rush—it takes time, and most importantly, it starts with learning to love ourselves.

If you've ever felt alone, if you've ever struggled to understand your own heart, know that you are not alone. I hope these pages remind you that love is not just about others, but about how we care for ourselves through every high and low. And no matter where you are in your journey, there is always hope for a new beginning.

Prologue

Sreehari K.N - writer and film enthusiast.

Holding a post-graduation in English Literature, he first found his voice through poetry and reflections shared on Instagram, where his words resonated with a wide audience. Over time, these writings evolved into published works a collection of poetry and a fiction novel marking his journey from digital expression to print.

Deeply passionate about cinema and literature, Sreehari's work explores themes of love, longing, and the intricacies of human emotions. *Where Do Our Hearts Go* is an extension of this journey, capturing the wandering echoes of the heart in lyrical form.

1. all my poetry was about you.

Nine Novembers Later,
You'll Know that all my poetry was about you."

2. Have you ever lost in love?

At one point, I felt completely alone and stuck between life and death after failing at love. Uncertain of how to go, I walked among the remains of what had been.

However, I managed to survive rather well. And as I write this now, I am overcome with thankfulness for that very love that I once lost. It was not just the end, but also the start of days of learning, relearning, and understanding my hidden potential.

3. You.!

"*I left pieces of me in you,*
and you in me.
Now, I search for myself,
in places only you knew."

4. Have you ever met someone who felt like home?

Some people enter your life and give you the warmth that you were lacking. Their presence feels like a familiar song. With them, silence is comfortable, and time moves differently. But not everyone who feels like home is meant to stay. Some are just passing through, leaving behind pieces of themselves while teaching and healing you. And perhaps that's okay!
Do you have a house, then?

5. what if

"You were my favorite what if,
the chapter I longed to rewrite.
But love isn't a second draft,
it's a story that ends when it must."

6. I thought I couldn't move on.

However, I now understand that the only way to truly grow was to move on.

For a long time, I believed that moving on would mean erasing what we had, that it would feel like forgetting. But in truth, moving on doesn't mean leaving the past behind it means stepping into the future. It means making space for new experiences, new loves, and new versions of myself. And with each step forward, I feel stronger, braver, and more alive than I've ever felt before.

7. Poem

"We met in the middle of a poem,
but never reached the final line."

8. Have you ever held on to something that was already gone?

It's a strange thing, clinging to a love that has already left. You replay old conversations, searching for signs you might have missed, as if understanding the past will change the present. You hold on to memories like they are lifelines, afraid to let go because you fear losing a part of yourself with them. But the truth is, what's meant to stay will stay. And what leaves was never truly yours to keep.

Letting go isn't forgetting, it's making space for something new.

9. Unspoken words

• 9 •

"

We spoke in unspoken words,
understood in silences deep.
But one day, the silence stretched too far,
and we lost what we couldn't keep. "

10. Have you ever loved someone in silence?

There is a kind of love that never finds its voice. A love that lingers in stolen glances, in words left unsaid, in the quiet ache of wanting but never reaching. It exists in the spaces between conversations, in the way your heart races when they are near, in the silent prayers you whisper just to see them happy. And though it never takes shape in the real world, it is no less real. **Some loves are meant to be felt, not spoken.**

11. Metaphors

"We met in poetry
and loved in metaphors
but real life never rhymed
the way we hoped."

12. Have you ever loved someone who couldn't love you back?

Loving someone who cannot love you back is like writing letters to an address that no longer exists. You pour yourself into them, hoping they will see you, feel you, need you the way you need them. But love isn't something that can be forced or earned it is either given freely or not at all. And so, you learn to love in silence, to cherish from a distance, and eventually, to let go.

13. Forever ?

You promised forever,
but forever was shorter than I thought.
Now, I count time in memories,
not in moments.

14. Have you ever loved someone in a way they never understood?

There is a quiet kind of love that exists in the unnoticed details **the way you remember their favorite songs,the way your heart softens when they laugh, the way you silently wish for their happiness**, even if it doesn't include you. It's the kind of love that never demands, never asks for anything in return. But sometimes, loving someone like that can feel like screaming into the void, hoping they'll hear what you never had the courage to say.

15. Just two hearts

"Our story ended softly,
no anger, no blame.
Just two hearts growing quieter,
until silence said it all."

16. It was hard to see the light some days

But I've learned that even the smallest spark can brighten the darkest room.

When the weight of responsibilities and the strain of family and work issues became too much,

it felt like I was living in constant shadow. There were moments when I didn't know how I would make it through the day. But I've come to realize that survival doesn't always require grand changes. Sometimes, it's the smallest moments of hope, of kindness, of resilience, that can keep us moving forward.

I don't need everything to be perfect. I just need the strength to find my spark. And that's enough.

17. Shelter

"You were my safest place,
until love turned into a storm.
Now, I stand in the wreckage,
wondering where the shelter went."

18. Have you ever held onto something that was already breaking?

There's a moment when you realize that no matter how tightly you hold on, things are already slipping away. You tell yourself that if you love harder, if you try more, if you change just enough, maybe you can stop the inevitable. But love isn't about holding on to something that hurts you. Sometimes, the bravest thing you can do is loosen your grip, let go, and trust that life will bring you something better.

19. Lighthouse

"Our love was a lighthouse,
steady and bright.
But you longed for the open sea,
and I couldn't make you stay on shore."

20. Have you ever been haunted by words left unsaid?

There are things I wish I had said, words that still sit heavy on my tongue, waiting for a moment that will never come. I should have told them how much they meant to me, how deeply they were loved. But sometimes, life moves too fast, and before we realize it, the moment has passed. And so, we carry those words, whisper them to the wind, hope that somehow, in some way, they will still be heard.

21. You walked out before the ending.

"We built a home in quiet verses,
a shelter made of unspoken dreams.
Yet the wind came whispering your name,
and you walked out before the ending."

22. It left with you

"You asked where my heart had gone,
but I never had the words to say
It left with you, long ago,
and never found its way back."

23. Some days, I felt like I was drowning.

But somehow, I kept my head above water.

The family tension, the job stress, the never-ending demands it felt like they were all pulling me down. There were times I thought I couldn't take any more, that I had reached my limit. But even in the darkest moments, I found a way to breathe.

I survived not by escaping my problems, but by facing them. By taking each challenge, each struggle, and breaking it down into something I could handle. One breath at a time. And in doing so, I found strength I never knew I had.

24. Ever felt like you're holding onto a dream that's slipping away?

There comes a time when you realize that no matter how much you want something, some dreams are not meant to be yours. You tell yourself to fight a little harder, to believe a little longer, but deep down, you know. And yet, letting go isn't easy. It's grieving a future you once imagined, learning to rewrite your story, and trusting that new dreams will find you when the time is right.

25. Love stood between us

"Love stood between us,
a river too wide to cross.
We watched it flow away,
carrying all we never said."

26. What if the love you lost was the love that saved you?

It's easy to think of lost love as failure, to believe that something so beautiful should have lasted forever. But sometimes, love comes not to stay, but to teach. It shows you the depths of your heart, the strength you never knew you had, the way endings can be beginnings in disguise. **The love that left shaped you, prepared you, and in some strange way, saved you.**

27. Does a part of you still belong to them?

They say time heals, but some loves don't fade they just settle in the corners of your heart, quiet but ever-present. You move on, you learn to smile again, but there are days when their name still lingers on your tongue, when an old song feels like an open wound. It's not that you want them back, but some people leave marks that time cannot erase. And maybe that's okay. Maybe we are meant to carry pieces of those we once loved.

28. What if the love was real, but the timing wasn't?

Not all love stories end because the love was lacking. Sometimes, two people meet when they are not ready to hold each other the way they should. Sometimes, love arrives too soon or too late, forcing you to walk away from something you still want. But the cruelest truth of all? Even the right love, at the wrong time, still breaks your heart the same

29. For the love we left untold.

"We wrote our story in borrowed time,
pages turning too fast to hold.
Now I search between the lines,
for the love we left untold."

30. I didn't know how long I could keep fighting.

But somewhere along the way, I realized the fight wasn't against life it was with myself.

The struggles with family expectations, the pressure to excel at work, the constant issues of responsibilities all of it felt like a heavy weight. I thought I was fighting the world, but I was really fighting my own fear, doubt, and insecurity. Once I stopped seeing life as a battle to win, I began to see it as a journey to survive, to learn, and to grow.

I'm still standing because I chose to believe in myself. And that belief is the one thing that no one can ever take away from me.

31. Without you

"There was a time when I thought
I couldn't live without you.
But here I am
breathing, healing, growing."

32. Where do broken hearts go?

The moon saw us together,
the sun saw us apart.
Now the stars only ask me,
where do broken hearts go?"

33. Maybe in another story

"We were pages torn from the same book,
scattered by time and fate.
Maybe in another story,
our words will meet again."

34. Letting go wasn't losing you

It was finding myself.

When we parted ways, I thought I was losing everything losing you, losing the future I imagined. But what I found was something even more powerful: myself. Letting go didn't mean giving up; it meant making space for the person I am meant to be. I am learning to walk this life with my own strength, to love myself with the same intensity I once loved you. And in that, I've found more joy, peace, and freedom than I ever imagined.

35. I thought I needed to be fixed

But now, I realize I was never broken.

For so long, I believed I was incomplete without you, that your love was the missing piece that would make me whole. But now, I see that I was never broken I was just learning. I don't need someone else to heal me; I have everything I need to heal myself. And in this self-love, I've found a power that no one can take away.

36. I thought I would always be afraid of being alone

But now, I've learned that solitude is where I find my strength. For so long, I feared being alone, thinking that without someone by my side, I wouldn't know who I was. But now, I understand that solitude is not something to fear; it is where I rediscover myself. It's in the silence that I find my strength, in the quiet moments that I hear my own heart. And now, I am no longer afraid of being alone, because I know I am enough, and I am all I need.

37. You taught me

Not all love stays,
But all love teaches.
And you,
You taught me how to love myself.

38. I thought I had nothing left

But now, I know I've only just begun.

When you left, I felt like the world had collapsed around me. But in the quiet of that space, I discovered something I hadn't realized before my journey wasn't over; it had just begun. I've begun to build myself up again, layer by layer, creating a life that is solely mine. I have everything I need to grow, to rise, and to become the person I've always been meant to be.

39. You left, and I stayed

And in staying, I found myself.

For a long time, I thought I had to leave with you to be happy, to be complete. But when you left, I realized that happiness isn't something you find in another person it's something you find within yourself. I stayed. And in staying, I realized that I don't need anyone else to feel whole. I am enough. My worth was never tied to your love; it was always tied to how I love and value myself.

40. You are still here

You are still here,
in songs I skip,
in places I avoid,
in the spaces you left behind.

41. I thought I needed you

• 41 •

But now, I see, I was always enough.

There was a time when I believed that love meant being incomplete without the other person, as if I couldn't be whole unless you were there to fill the empty spaces in me. I put so much of myself into you, trying to find meaning in your affection. But now, in the quiet after you've gone, I've realized something I never truly understood before I was always enough. The love I thought I needed from you was already inside me, waiting to be uncovered.

42. I no longer

"I no longer wait for your message,
no longer search for your name.
I have learned to be happy
without needing a reminder."

43. I thought losing you would break me.

But now, I know it was the start of my healing.

In the beginning, it felt like the end of everything. Losing you left a hole in me, and for a long time, I thought I couldn't move forward without you. But with every passing day, I see that your absence is not an emptiness it is the space I needed to heal. Losing you wasn't my end. It was the beginning of something new. It's the start of discovering who I am without the weight of holding on.

44. Losing you..

It's not a relief, not a victory. It's simply the truth. The love I once held for you has faded, not because I stopped caring, but because I grew into something new. And now, that space where you once lived is filled with me. I'm no longer waiting for something to return. I'm standing on my own, and for the first time, I realize that this is enough.

45. I thought I couldn't move on.

But now, I know moving on means moving forward, not forgetting.

At first, the idea of moving on felt impossible. How could I move forward when part of me was still holding onto what we had? But now I realize that moving on doesn't mean erasing you from my heart it means making room for myself to grow. It means embracing the lessons, the strength, and the beauty that came from our time together, and using them to become the best version of myself.

46. Cage..

"I thought I would always love you,
but love isn't meant to be a cage.
One day, I walked out
and never looked back."

47. I thought I wasn't enough

I thought I wasn't enough.

But now, I know I am more than enough.

In the past, I questioned my worth, wondering why I wasn't enough for you. But now, I see that I was never meant to fit into someone else's definition of love. I am enough as I am strong, beautiful, and whole. I no longer seek validation outside of myself because I know my own value. I am learning to love myself in ways I never thought possible, and that love is all I need

48. I don't love you anymore

49. Your heart will find its light.

"As the last words of this journey unfold,
I realize that healing isn't just about moving on it's about becoming. Becoming someone who understands the depth of their own heart, someone who learns to love with all the pieces they've gathered, broken or whole. Through the pain, the loneliness, the longing, I've learned that the most profound love comes not from another person, but from within. This journey has taught me that even in our most fragile moments, we are capable of becoming something beautiful, something stronger than we ever imagined. And though the road has been long, and the scars are still here, I carry them with pride, because they are part of the story that makes me who I am.

So, to you, dear reader, wherever you are on your journey never forget that you are worthy of love. Hold on to the belief that every ending is a new beginning, and even in the darkest of times, your heart will find its light.

- With Love Sreeeeeeeee....."

50. All my poetry was about you !

"Nine Novembers Later,
We'll meet again...
and laugh over how different
our lives turned out to be !
I'd wish if I could've been brave
enough to say the things I was
too afraid to say and to feel.
The things I was afraid to feel !
Nine novembers later,
I'll pretend to have forgotten
How your lips form creases
when you smile,
How those soulful eyes squint.
When you talk and the mole
by your left chin.
Nine Novembers Later,
You'll know that all my poetry
was about You..!!

- Anu Anna...."